The For Sale by Owner Handbook

The For Sale by Owner Handbook

Your Step-by-Step Solution

to Marketing and Selling

Your Home on Your Own

Pierre Mouchette, author

The For Sale by Owner Handbook

ISBN 13: 978-1540896865
ISBN 10: 1540896862
Printed in the United States of America

"This publication is designed to provide accurate and authoritative information regarding the subject matter covered. It is sold with the understanding that the publisher is not engaged in rendering legal, accounting, or other professional advice. If legal advice or other expert assistance is required, the services of a competent professional person should be sought." (From a *Declaration of Principles* jointly adopted by a committee of the American Bar Association and a committee of publishers and associations.)

Library of Congress Control Number: 2016920560
CreateSpace Independent Publishing Platform, North Charleston, SC

This book is dedicated to the homeowner.

Taking a house and then turning it into a home

is a special task of love.

My best wishes to you in selling your home!

Contents

Preface

The For Sale by Owner Handbook will provide readers with useful information on preparing to market and sell their homes.

The book is written in an easy-to-read format for instant implementation.

Section 1   GETTING STARTED

1.0   The Opportunity

Many homeowners are taking advantage of today's rebounding real estate market to sell their homes without the services of a real estate professional. *The For Sale by Owner Handbook* will help homeowners to sell their homes through the use of advanced marketing techniques and tools.

1.1   The Market

For most homeowners, trying to sell their homes without the services of a real estate professional (and that 5 to 6 percent fee) is not an option but a necessity. Probably having bought your home within the last eight years, you now find that your home does not have the resale value that you had anticipated and is worth a lot less than what you purchased it for. This is called *being upside down*.

1.2   The Assessment

If you have decided to undertake the task of selling your own home, we suggest that you take paper and pencil and evaluate the home, from the outside to the inside.

Here are our make-ready suggestions:

a) Exterior make-ready
   o   Cut grass, trim perimeter, and remove weeds.
   o   Trim all shrubbery and, if necessary, "umbrella" the trees.
   o   Spread mulch as required.
   o   Power wash the building's exterior.
b) Interior make-ready

o   Make-ready cleaning: Clean all areas of the home with ammonia and warm water. Basically, the following should be cleaned:

Entrance	Clean front door inside and out.
Kitchen	Clean all appliances inside and out. Clean sides of, behind, and underneath refrigerator and stove. Clean inside all drawers, cabinets, and pantries. Clean vent hood and replace filter. Replace drip pans on stove as necessary. Clean and oil cabinets. Clean and polish sinks, faucets, and countertops. Replace faucet washers. Clean faucet aerator and flow restrictor. Replace light bulbs.
Bathroom	Clean and polish sink, tub, and toilet. Clean and polish faucet, spout, and shower diverter. Replace faucet washers. Clean faucet aerator and flow restrictor. Clean shower-head flow restrictor. Clean and polish tiles. Clean and polish countertop and mirrors. Clean inside all drawers and cabinets. Clean and polish all light fixtures and vents. Replace light bulbs.
Misc.	Sweep, mop, and polish all floors. Vacuum all carpeting. Shampoo carpeting. Clean closet shelves and rods. Clean windows inside and out.

> Clean light fixtures.
> Replace all switch plates and outlet covers with new ones.
> Clean A/C vents.
> Clean outside porch light fixture and replace bulb.
> Sweep porch, patio/balcony, and storage areas.
> Clean ceiling fans and replace all bulbs.
> Clean fireplace.

o Make-ready painting: Any area that cannot be spruced up with a good cleaning (soap and water) should be repainted in a neutral color. A good paint job will transform a "well lived in home" into the look and detail of a "custom home."

o Complete the following before painting:

- Remove all outlet covers and switch plates.
- Sweep baseboards.
- Spackle all nail holes.
- Molding and trim, A/C grills.
- Closet and closet rods.
- Exterior doors, interior doors, outside storage room doors.
- Hallway, living room, kitchen, bathroom.

o Make-ready maintenance: Ensure that everything is in perfect working condition.

- Make ready (replace as required)
- Doors (threshold, weather strip, doorstop, doorbell, keys)
- Vent hood

- Cabinet doors (knobs, hinges, friction catches)
- Kitchen countertops
- Kitchen floor
- Kitchen sink (faucets, O-rings, seats, washers, aerators, trap, drain)
- Disposal
- Dishwasher
- Stove (burners)
- Oven (element, broiler pan)
- Refrigerator (crisper, glass, meat tray, door seal, ice trays)
- Bathroom floor
- Water closet (ballcock, flush, bowl, seat)
- Lavatory (trap, drain, pop-up, O-ring, seat, washer)
- Tissue holder
- Towel racks
- Bathtub (stopper, pop-up, tile, grout, valves, O-ring, seat, washer, shower head, soap dish)
- Bathroom cabinets (door, drawer)
- AC (filter, knob, cooling)
- Heat
- Windows (locks, screens)
- Miniblinds/drapes (rod, cord)
- Outlets
- Switches
- Molding and trim
- Wall covering
- Sheetrock, walls, ceiling
- Fireplace
- Caulk (remove old caulk and recaulk as needed)

c) Final
   o Door locks
   o Keyless bolting device
   o Sliding door lock, latch

- o Window locks
- o Smoke detectors (replace batteries)
- o Intrusion alarm
- o Fire extinguisher (check dates)

1.3 The Unveiling

Now that you have your home spic and span, it's almost time for the next step. Remember: you must keep your home in this condition until you sell it!

Most buyers are impulsive and want to preview your home with a moment's notice. In the appendix, we present a solution that may help with this problem called **Talking House**.

Section 2   The Marketplace

2.0   The Marketplace

Most Realtors offer a free service in that they will research the market value of your home for free. This is an excellent opportunity for you to have a few Realtors come in and give you their impressions of what your home is worth. Since this price is subjective, ask them for comparable homes in your area. If they are professional, they will put together a complete package that will give you a lot of insight into the marketplace and your home.

In addition to the above, you can go online and get estimates for free at these sites:

Zillow   http://www.zillow.com

Home Pages   http://www.homepages.com

Online Home Values   http://www.online-home-values.com

2.1   The Realtor

Meeting with Realtors also serves as a future strategy. If—and I say only *if*—you cannot sell the home on your own, you will have already made contacts with real estate professionals, and you will know how they present themselves and their companies and what they can do for you.

2.2   Pricing Your Home

We all want to get the maximum dollar on the sale of our homes. Armed with the information from the Realtors, you can calculate what the market will pay on this date for your home. **Caution:** If you overprice the home, it will not sell fast, and the market can change. Another thought is that buyers assume that they can discount what a Realtor would have received (as commission) if you had listed your home with one, so they will always try to start with an offer below your asking price.

Now to pricing:

- Call the lender (bank) and ask for a payoff balance as of what date (should be the first day of the following month).
- Subtract the payoff from what the Realtor said your house is worth on the open market.

This will give you an **idea** of what you can clear after the sale.

2.3   Upside Down

Sometimes owing to market or other conditions, we cannot sell our homes for what we feel they should sell for. In this case, if you are forced to move (e.g., for a job), a good solution is to rent the home out! You can use the Realtor as the management company.

Section 3   Prepare to Show

3.0   Preparation

Now you must prepare for the multitude of people who will be banging down your door for the opportunity to see and make an offer on your home.

3.1   The Tools

These are the tools for selling your home:

- Telephone with answering machine
- Pen and paper
- Questionnaire: The following are some questions that you might ask when receiving calls about your home to establish a dialog with callers and find out how you can best sell them your home. (Use discretion when asking these questions.)
  - How did you hear about (or who referred you to) me?
  - What is your name and phone number?
  - What is your home address?
  - Do you currently own a home?
  - Do you expect to sell or rent your present home?
  - Have you purchased a home before?
  - How long have you been shopping for a home?
  - Are you currently working with a Realtor?
  - Have you been prequalified for a mortgage amount?
  - Are you preapproved for a mortgage?
  - What features are you looking for in your new home?
    - Single family, multifamily, townhouse, or condominium
    - Location
    - Size (square footage, number of bedrooms)
    - Size of lot

- Finished basement
- Condition/age of home
- Unique features
  o What geographic areas are you considering?
  o Are there any questions that I can answer for you regarding the home purchase price?
  o Have you made the decision to purchase?

3.2   Your Attorney

State and federal law require that sellers provide specific documents and disclosures to home buyers; these are normally provided by the real estate agent. If these documents are not provided, it could result in costly and unnecessary litigation between a buyer and seller after the sale of the home.

Speak with your **attorney**, and obtain from him all the necessary paperwork!

Section 4 Advertising

4.0 The Buyer

Now that you have prepared your home for sale, the question arises: How do you do it? The answer is simple: you must make **buyers** aware of the fact that your home is available and that you are ready, willing, and able to sell.

4.1 The Media

Newspapers and Craigslist are the two most popular media used for the advertising of **homes for sale**. How you write up the notice often sells your audience.

4.2 Yard Sign

The yard sign can attract anyone who is driving through your neighborhood, or it can direct them to your door by sight.

4.3 Other Means

A lot of home sellers and real estate agents have had a lot of success with an electronic device called **Talking House**. Here's how it works: A curbside sign tells passersby to tune their car radios to a certain station. When they do, a VCR-sized transmitter in your home tells them all the best-selling features. This Talking House system is pure gold because it

- pulls prospects to the curbside of your home;
- reveals your home's very best features; and

- discourages strangers from knocking on your door without appointments, because it instructs passersby to call, not knock.

This system makes so much sense. Imagine how quickly you could sell your home if you had time to stand outside all day and night and explain its best features. Well, thanks to Talking House, you can!

Section 5   The Buyer

5.0   The Buyer

Now that everything is in place, you hungrily await your **buyer**. Of utmost importance is to remember that the buyer has a mind-set that your property is at least 10 percent overpriced (5 percent Realtor commission and 5 percent negotiating).

5.1   Buyer Preparation

In preparation for the **buyer**, as a well-informed **seller** (you purchased this book, didn't you?) of real property, you have prepared the following:

- The exterior of your home is in fantastic condition (section 1).
- The interior of your home looks like a finely polished gem with everything in its place (section 1).
- You have studied the marketplace and know the market value of real property in your neighborhood (section 2).
- You have priced your home according to the marketplace, without emotion (section 2).

Now the buyer has entered your web, by appointment, and you are ready!

5.2   The Table

Upon answering the bell, you heartily welcome the buyers into your home, thanking them for coming (while walking them to the foyer table). At the table, you pause and place in their hands a brochure (see Appendix B) of your home.

Don't forget to log them in the **showing log.**

5.3 The Showing

Walk buyers through your home, and tell them the following (you should have rehearsed this a hundred times so that it flows from you):

- Why you chose the house
- What improvements you have made
- About your neighbors and, if they have children, about children on the block
- About shopping and public transportation

5.4 The Closing

Thank the buyers for coming to your home. Ask if there is anything that you may have forgotten to tell them. Ask whether they have any questions.

Again, tell them to call if they think of anything on their way home that you can answer.

5.5 The Sale

When buyers call to tell you that they are interested in making an offer on your home, *thank them for making a wise decision*, and invite them back to your home.

When meeting with buyers for offers, be ready with the following:

- Know your bottom line, negotiate, negotiate, and negotiate!
- Go down in small numbers.
- Do not give it away in one shot; let them work hard at the table for it!

When you agree on a final number:

- Bring out the disclosures your attorney gave you;
- Have them sign that they received the disclosures;
- Have them sign the offer to purchase.

Congratulate **them** *on making a good deal, and say that you will miss the home, but unfortunately you have to sell because of whatever reason.*

Make a copy of the Statement of Understanding and give it to them. Tell them that it is a reminder, and congratulate them again.

Statement of Understanding

(What NOT to Do after You Apply for a Mortgage)

Congratulations! You finally found the house of your dreams. You made a bid, had it accepted by the seller, and went through the mortgage application process. It looks as if you will qualify. The closing is only weeks away, and you are feeling good.

It is smooth sailing from here, right? Probably. However, more than one buyer has had the wind knocked out of his sails at some point in a real estate transaction by the missteps described below. If possible, avoid the following no-no's until after you have gone to closing.

- ***Do not take on new debt.*** The temptation is strong. There are so many big purchases that people want to make in connection with a move: appliances, window treatments, furniture, and so on. When you add to this the fact that today everyone offers easy terms and no money down, well, why not just do it? Answer: Because you will change what the mortgage industry calls your debt-to-income ratio (the relationship of your income to your debt).

- ***Do not change jobs.*** If possible, try not to make a career move during the time between your mortgage application and the closing on the home you are purchasing. But you ask, "What if it's a better job, for more money, in a different field?" Still, try to wait until after closing. One of the factors mortgage companies consider is length of present employment; they are partial to stability. At the very least, changing jobs initiates the need for more paperwork and may delay your closing.

- ***Do not pack too soon.*** Well, go ahead and pack your clothes and dishes. But do not pack your bank statements, tax returns, or other important paperwork. Most especially, do not pack your checkbook! More than one buyer has had closing delayed while a friend or relative hurried over with additional funds because the checkbook was in the moving van.

- ***Do not lease a car.*** This should go under the general heading of "no new debt." It is highlighted here because for some strange reason, many buyers run right out and lease a new car during the time between mortgage application and closing! As with any debt, this will change your debt-to-income ratio and may cause you not to qualify for your mortgage.

In short, do nothing that negatively affects your ability to qualify for your mortgage loan or initiate a new round of paperwork. If you have any doubts about doing something that may affect your ability to qualify for your mortgage loan, please consult your loan provider before you do it.

These suggestions are merely that: suggestions. No one is saying, flat out, that bad things will necessarily follow if you do any of the above. They are offered as cautions. Many buyers seem to view the mortgage application procedure as a static action, a snapshot of their financial lives at a given moment in time. It is not. It's an ongoing process that considers everything you do right up until the day of closing.

The For Sale by Owner Handbook

Appendix A
Commonly Used Words and Phrases

Commonly Used Words and Phrases

Word or phrase	Meaning
Abatement	A reduction or decrease.
Ad valorem	A Latin phrase meaning "according to value." An assessment of taxes against a property according to its value.
Agent	One who acts for and with authority from another, called the *principal*.
Agreement	An exchange of promises, a mutual understanding or arrangement, or a contract. *All agreements must be in writing and acknowledged by all parties.*
Allowance	A sum of money set aside in the contract for items that have not been selected and named in the contract.
Appraisal	An opinion of the value of property resulting from an analysis of facts about the property.
Appraiser	An individual qualified by education, training, and experience who is hired to estimate the value of real property based on experience, judgment, facts, and use of formal appraisal processes.
Appreciation	An increase in the value of property due to changes in market conditions, inflation, or other causes.

Assessor	A public official who establishes the value of property for taxation purposes.
Binder	A deposit by the buyer to purchase the home according to the terms of the contract.
Borrowers	Individuals, revocable trusts, and LLCs.
Certificate of occupancy	This certificate is issued by the local government jurisdiction after all inspections have been made and approved on the building. Until the certificate of occupancy is issued, the homeowner cannot move in.
Change order	A written document that modifies the home's original features, floor plan, or finishes. Change orders usually add to the price of the home and may require additional time to complete.
Conditions, covenants, and restrictions (CC&Rs)	The standards that define how a property may be used and the protections made by the developer or homeowners' association that must be followed by all residents in the master-planned community.
Contingencies	A condition that the buyer makes as a condition of sale. Any contingency must have a date to be satisfied by and a statement as to what happens if it is not satisfied.
Contingency (financing)	Period of time for the buyer to acquire financing.
Executed contract	Contracts that are signed by all parties, sometimes referred to as *signed-in-*

	counterpart.
Extras	Work the buyer requests the contractor to do that is not in the contract but will be billed separately.
Fair market value	The highest price that a buyer who is willing, but not compelled, to buy would pay and the lowest a seller who is willing, but not compelled, to sell would accept.
Implied warranty	All states require builders to offer an implied warranty on their homes regardless of whether they also offer a written warranty. The implied warranty means that the builder is held responsible for repairing its work for a certain period of time.
Impounds	The lender will escrow taxes and insurance.
Manufacturer's specifications	Written installation and/or maintenance instructions provided by a product's manufacturer that must be followed to maintain the product's warranty.
Mortgage	A legal document that pledges a property to the lender as security for payment of a debt. The mortgage is a lien on the property. Instead of mortgages, some states use first trust deeds.
Note	A legal document that obligates a borrower to repay a mortgage loan at a stated interest rate during a specified period of time.
Payment	A schedule agreed upon before the start of construction of a custom house, starting with

schedule	a deposit and tied to the progress being made.
Penalty clause	A clause in the contract that provides for a reduction in payment to the contractor or his sub if deadlines are missed or the house is not completed according to specifications.
Performance bond	Funds, usually 10 percent of the total contract price, that the contractor must deposit as an insurance policy to guarantee the contractor's proper and timely completion.
Permit	Required authorization from a government authority to build a house or proceed with a phase of the building process.
Plot plan	A plan provided by a surveyor that shows the location of the house on the lot and also includes easements, property lines, required setbacks, and legal descriptions.
Punch list	A list created to show items that need to be fixed or that are missing.
Rate caps	This states the interest rate charge cannot change more than a specified amount during the life of the loan.
Real property	Land and appurtenances, including anything of a permanent nature, such as structures, trees, and minerals and the interest, benefits, and inherent rights thereof.

Appendix B
Seller Sales Aids

The Brochure

1. Your brochure should consist of a nice folder similar to a
   a. twin-pocket portfolio or
   b. Show File Presentation Book.
2. The contents should include the following:
   a. Photographs of
      i. the interior of the home,
      ii. the exterior of the home, and
      iii. the block
   b. A copy of the field card from the town hall
   c. A narrative telling about the home's highlights

The Narrative (no more than 8.5 × 11 inches)

Example

259 Pond Road, West Norwalk, CT

Unique property with fireplace in family rm., living rm., dining rm., 14 × 13 ground-level deck, mud rm. (10 × 8), first-floor master BR, 3-car attached garage, and in-ground swimming pool. Basement has partial finished room, sitting room, and unfinished area of 22 × 8.

Single-family residential

Rooms: 8

Bedrooms: 4

Baths: 2 full / 1 half

Laundry

Full basement

Included in sale: washer/dryer, stove, refrigerator, dishwasher

Colonial built 1993

3-car attached garage

Approx. 4,110 sq. ft.

3.01 acres

Gas warm-air heating

Central air

Est. taxes $8,292

Assessment $358,350

Sales Aids

Make the following sales aids to help you in marketing your home:

- *Daily call log and showing log*. Enter into your log all the people who inquire or even show up at your door. Be sure to record all their information so that you can follow up with them.

- *Results log*. This will help you keep track of how many calls you receive and from what source. By keeping an accurate record, you will know which source provides the greatest return on your advertising dollar.

The For Sale by Owner Handbook

Daily Call Log

Date: _____

	Name	Address	Telephone	Showing date	Showing time	Notes
1						
2						
3						
4						
5						
5						
6						

Instructions: Enter caller name, address, and telephone number. Give a brief description of the home, and set up a showing date and time. Enter any appropriate notes.

Daily Showing Log

Date: _____

	Name	Address	Telephone	Showing time	Notes
1					
2					
3					
4					
5					
5					
6					

Instructions: Enter caller name, address, and telephone number.
Give a brief description of the home, and set up a showing date and time.
Enter any appropriate notes.

Showing Results Log

Date: _____

	Name	Address	Telephone	Results
1				
2				
3				
4				
5				
5				
6				

Instructions: Enter caller name, address, and telephone number.

The For Sale by Owner Handbook

Contact Results Log

Date: _____

Sources	Sun	Mon	Tue	Wed	Thur	Fri	Total	Comments
Walk-ins								
Newspaper								
Flyers								
Word of mouth								
Friends								
Talking House								
Other								
Daily total								

Appendix C
Talking House

Talking House FAQs

Q: What is Talking House?

A: Talking House is an easy-to-operate, low-power AM radio transmitter that a Realtor or home seller can use to broadcast prerecorded advertising messages to cars as they stop outside a home for sale. Users simply record a message using a handheld microphone and put the transmitter inside the home. They can hide it in a closet or even the attic and plug it in. They can set up the whole system in less than ten minutes. A yard sign instructs home shoppers to tune to a specific radio frequency as they stop in front of a home. They hear all about the unique features of that specific home without leaving the comfort of their car!

Q: How big is the transmitter?

A: The Talking House transmitter is about the size of a small VCR. The transmitter weighs only four pounds and operates on standard 120-volt AC power.

Q: What do the messages typically say?

A: Talking House can be used to answer many of the routine questions, and some of the not-so-routine questions, that a home buyer has about a home, such as the following:

- How many bedrooms and bathrooms?
- What's the square footage?

- Are there hardwood floors?
- Is there a fireplace?
- How big is the master bath?
- How big is the lot, especially the backyard?

Because the voice recording is done on a digital chip, the message can be changed as often as you like. The message can be up to five minutes in length. Because it's digital, there is never any denigration in its quality. The message will just repeat in a loop twenty-four hours a day, seven days a week. Therefore, Talking House is on the job promoting the house 365 days a year, nonstop.

Q: Where does the transmitter go?

A: The transmitter can be placed almost anywhere inside a home. It is safe, silent, and nonintrusive. Installation takes only ten minutes. Moreover, Talking House will not interfere with other radio stations or with any other electronic equipment in the home or in nearby neighborhoods.

Q: What kind of antenna is used?

A: The basic antenna is an eight-foot-long rubberized wire. With a signal range averaging more than three hundred feet, Talking House can deliver a crisp, clear radio signal to drivers listening while parked on the street in front of a home. Signal range will vary with installation style and environmental factors such as line of sight and other interference.

Q: Is Talking House easy to use?

A: Yes, the message is loaded onto a five-minute digital chip simply by speaking into the handheld microphone. Or a professionally produced message can be downloaded using a cassette or CD player. The message can be any length up to five minutes, without any dead air, and can be changed as often as you like. Because it's digital, there is never any denigration in quality.

Q: Is a license required?

A: No, the FCC under Part 15 of its radio regulations authorizes Talking House (FCC Identification #DLB5LTT98.) Its users do not require a separate license. Talking House broadcasts on any frequency on the entire AM band (560 to 1700 AM).

Specifications

Transmitter

- Range: 300 feet (varies with installation style and environmental factors)
- Frequency choices: 560–1700 AM
- Message length: up to 5 minutes
- Message storage: nonvolatile computer chips
- Microphone: built-in and handheld
- Dimensions: 8" × 14" × 2.5"
- Weight: 4 lb.
- Power: 110 V AC / 12 V DC
- Antenna: 3 meters
- Final input power: 100 MW average
- Frequency control: crystal with synthesizer
- Mounting: varies with installation type—external antenna available

Power Supply

- Input power requirements: 115 V AC, 60 Hz, 0.1 amp
- Output voltage: 12 V DC, 0.2 amp

www.ingramcontent.com/pod-product-compliance
Lightning Source LLC
Chambersburg PA
CBHW061233180526
45170CB00003B/1276